HUBCAP
COLLECTION
PLATE

Also by JEFFREY DUNN

Novels

Dream Fishing the Little Spokane

Radio Free Olympia

A Whiskey Rebel from Moses Coulee
 (coming 2023)

When Wildcat Changed (coming 2024)

Poetry

The Belfast Bodhisattva

No Name Lake Coronach

Cup of Joe

Literary Criticism

William S. Burroughs and Technologizing
 Literature in the Industrial Age

HUBCAP COLLECTION PLATE

by

JEFFREY DUNN

Inchitensee
Spokane

Published in 2022 by Inchitensee
11707 North Waikiki Road
Spokane, WA 99218
inchitensee@gmail.com

Distributed by IngamSpark

COVER and THE BELFAST BODHISATTVA
photograph by Beck Shepherd 2018.
Courtesy of the photographer.

First Printing

*This book is for
sound and passion
everywhere.*

CONTENTS

Cup of Joe

Gratitude

Call it Portrait of an Artist as an Old Man in celebration of the great modern Irishman, James Joyce, who told a story about Stephen, the youth who chose the word lineage of the artist upon which to construct his own creative self. Not the priest. Not the politician.

Or call it The Ferlinberger Blue Plate Special because "Ferlinberger" celebrates Lawrence Ferlinghetti, especially his poem "Autobiography," and Allen Ginsberg, especially his poem "Howl"—language well-springs all, eh? in much the same way we come back to diner meals served on blue plates, often in Blue Willow pattern, divided into sections: one for meatloaf, one for fried potatoes, and one for fresh-from-the-can carrots—all turned as one into American muscle-bones, American cities of gods, American dreams, American choke-cherry pie in the sky.

Gratitude to Charles Baudelaire, Allen
　　Ginsberg, and Lawrence Ferlinghetti.
Gratitude to William Carlos Williams, Walt
　　Whitman, and William Blake.
Gratitude to John Kennedy and Karl Marx.
Gratitude to Richard Brautigan, Gary
　　Snyder, and Jack Kerouac.
Gratitude to Thomas Wolfe, Carl Sandberg,
　　and Stephen Crane.
Gratitude to Curt Kirkwood, Mike Brewer,
　　and Tom Shipley.
Gratitude to Patti Smith, Don Van Vliet,
　　and William S. Burroughs.
Gratitude to Ian Anderson, Otis Redding,

and Steve Cropper.
Gratitude to Amy Ray, Emily Saliers, and
all Riot Grrrls great and small.
Gratitude to John Lennon, Paul
McCartney, and Arthur Rimbaud.
Gratitude to Roky Erickson, Chris Cornell,
and Arthur Dodgson.
Gratitude to Walter Reynolds, Maximilien
Robespierre, and Diggers everywhere.
Gratitude to Sidney Clare, Harry
McClintock, Utah Phillips, and all folk
and spiritual musicians.

I

I am growing old with a cup of joe.
I am looking through the plate glass of the
    Blast Off Bakery at a crumbling
    concrete pillar supporting America's
    sclerotic arteries.
I am a maker, a teacher, and a shaker.
I am a Christian.
I am Buddhist.
I am a Marxist.
And I am a Citizen of the World.

I was born among the best minds of a
    previous generation and a Buster
    Brown shoe box shooting through the
    purple haze at the darker side of a
    failed intervention.
I was baptized in holy water from the River
    Jordan, and Sunday Schooled on the
    catechism of predestination.
I sat on the floor of education's hallowed
    halls, put my head between my knees,
    and kissed my ever-lovin' ass goodbye.
I was sent home from school because the
    President was dead, and my untutored,
    angelic mind wondered if that was
    good.
I was served t.v. dinners on t.v. trays in
    front of black and white, righteous
    family-hour broadcasts with the June
    Taylor dancers spread out like some
    chrysanthemum of femininity calling
    to Blakean intimations of puberty.
I completed jigsaw puzzles of Rockwellian
    Americana while Harlem and Bed-Stuy
    burned, brother Evers was shot dead,
    Elmo Lewis died at the bottom of a

pool; Watts burned, brother Malcolm
was shot dead, the Kozmic Pearl got
smacked; Newark burned, brother
Martin was shot dead, Jimi James
mixed bennies and jesus juice, threw
up, and drowned; Detroit burned,
brother Robert was shot dead, and the
Lizard King lost his Texas Radio signal,
the doors of perception slammed shut
in his face.
I was asked not what my country can do for
me, but what I can do to maximize the
return on my investments derived from
the sweat of America's workers, the
bodies of America's women, and the
tears of America's children.
And I sit benevolently, eyes wide open.

II

I am growing old with a cup of joe.
I am looking through the plate glass of the
      Chic-A-Go-Go at eleven perps and
      vices.
I take the Pepsi challenge, only care enough
      to send the very best, and see the
      U.S.A. in my Chevrolet.
I am all that I can be.
I wonder, "Where's the beef?"
I know Coke is the real thing.
And I am every innocent child who will
      someday be President.

I was raised on the breath of Pittsburgh's
      hookahs stoked with brimstone torn
      from Mother Earth's bowels deep
      inside West Virginia's innocent curves.
I watched unfeeling coal cars, like
      overburdened pack mules, like a fire
      brigade, like the sins of the fathers
      stretching all the way to the Damn
      Shame Mine, roll over trestles and
      through tunnels, disgorging into heart-
      of-darkness, celtic cauldrons.
I collected eggs and sausage in the summer
      steam of Cleveland's West Side Market
      and felt Artis the Spoonman's
      vibrations in the winter mist of
      Seattle's Pike Place Market.
I tended a nabemono of Denver sukiyaki
      and was visited by the Holy Goof.
I grilled fillets of Quinault blueback as the
      sun set over Huck Finn's sea of the
      dead.
I stuck my toes in the glacial melt running
      down the Dosewalips River and over

the passenger pigeon, Tacoma pocket
gopher, and Columbia Basin pygmy
rabbit.
I took a bite of bear sausage loaf on turkey
day and was mortal-sin afraid.
I pledged allegiance to the flag of tightening
my Indiana corn belt, putting on my
Seattle emerald glasses, and laying my
head on Chicago's broad shoulders; to
the flag of the shag-balls Willie Mays
flipped into beer-sticky stands; to the
flag of running up the down escalator
all to see through the eyes of park
bench winos; to the flag of Maury
Wills stealing my base, Farrah Fawcett
stealing my heart, and Patty Hearst
stealing my attention; to the flag of the
promotional poster displaying Cat
Ballou's cleavage; to the flag of the
moonscape rubble and pothole lakes of
the channeled scablands; and to the
flags of the Douglas-fir, Sitka spruce,
Western redcedar, ponderosa pine, and
lodgepole pine, although the subalpine,
silver, and noble firs still seem all one
flag to me.
I ate free dessert while gazing from the
Windows on the World atop the World
Trade Center only later to find that
Humpty Dumpty had a great fall all
because no honest man was found.
And I sit benevolently, eyes wide open.

III

I am growing old with a cup of joe.
I am looking through the plate glass
    window of the Sun Kids' Library at all
    that depends upon the white waterfall
    spanned by stone bridges next to the
    homeless camp.
I am a realist, a thinker, and a fabulist.
I am an urban Romantic.
I am a backwoods Modernist.
I am a classical Dadaist.
And I am every starving, great American
    novelist.

I took a copy of *On the Road* in my back
    pocket to Lusk, Wyoming, twice if you
    must know, and watched teen lust in
    cars pass by a rattler curled in the
    gutter, its elliptical eyes looking
    homeward angel.
I hiked with my trusty *Baudelaire Field
    Guide* above Capon Springs, West
    Virginia to ID ghost plants, painted
    turtles, and bloodroot.
I went to the plateau to find water, shoot
    guns, raise rabbits, and go one toke
    over the line with Jesus.
I ordered a beefheart sandwich with the
    Captain, a naked lunch with the heavy
    metal kids, and seven slices of brown
    toast with mapplethorpe syrup and
    black coffee.
I ascended the twelve Naropa stairs, held up
    my purring cat to the moon, and
    invoked stone-cold mountain spirits to
    come down and break the dharma over
    our top-down, land-filled, flame-

broiled selves.

I earned the red badge of philosophy after
     having scaled the ivory tower, and after
     reaching the summit, looked out over
     what counts for knowledge and
     determined I was but atop an ivory
     tower.

I sat on a dock by the bay and watched
     Daisy's green light blink away.

I crowded amongst 40,000 ears and heard
     80,000 watts all the while wondering
     aloud again.

I attended Olympia's Homo a GoGo bathed
     in the complete bareass release of
     America's love juices all twisted and
     shouted.

I felt the phallus within burn to ash and be
     replaced by fields of fireweed releasing
     hundreds-of-thousands of fluffy-flagged
     riot grrrl seeds.

I was nudged by Allen Ginsberg who said to
     me, "Let's make them nuts," as he
     proceeded to snap pictures of Lyndon
     LaRouche supporters promoting the
     colonization of Mars, all the while the
     Larouche supporters snapping back.

I crossed the boards of America's covered
     bridges and from the other side
     watched them get doused with napalm
     and thermite, making thirteen billion
     psychedelic camppyres.

And I sit benevolently, eyes wide open.

IV

I am growing old with a cup of joe.
I am looking through the plate glass
    window of the Channeled Scabland
    Operahouse at the mother of all
    haboobs to end all haboobs.
I am two dollars and twentyseven cents, a
    spider exploding across the stars, and
    un autre terrible.
I am a walrus.
I am thick as a brick.
I am a two-headed dog.
And I am every trumpet at the end of time.

I went down to the Little Pucketos Creek
    and searched for crawdads, shiners,
    chubs, hogsuckers, and mudpuppies, all
    the while singing songs of innocence to
    the wooly embrace of the maternal
    mysterion.
I combed Pacific beaches for oysters and
    dug for horse and littleneck clams, but
    especially for razor clams, frying them
    in butter so rich that angels are
    incarnated for less.
I tunneled for geoducks, gone deep, out-of-
    reach, into the sands of the great Pacific
    unconscious.
I was nourished on skipjacks, big macs, and
    slippery jacks, all warmed on a lunch
    counter under a blackhole sun.
I walked through Stumptown, America
    after the ax man's blade cut loose
    liberté, egalité, fraternité.
I entered into lives of urban, rural, and any-
    other-kind of renewal restoring an old
    lineman's lamp, filling it with

watermelontrout oil, and lighting it to
become the largest of fireflies, the
cicadas thrumming mad wilderness sex
rhythms the whole night through.
I sat with a Lon Chaney grin on Alice's
mushroom cloud.
I had a cool cranberry, sphinx-winged brain
cluttered with deadhead roses.
I rousted up some coffee cans and filled
them with free-to-the-people digger
bread using a recipe that went
something like this:

BREAD RECIPE from the
FREE BAKERY
one loaf in a 2-lb can
two loaves in 1-lb cans

WET MIXTURE
½ cup warm water
1 cake or package of yeast
1 tablespoon flour
1 tablespoon honey, molasses

DRY MIXTURE
1 level 1-lb coffee can whole-
wheat flour
2 teaspoons salt
¼ to ½ cup dry milk

I quaked under metallic blue angels casting
shadows in synchronous formation
across the innocent landscape and
ruffling the wool of unshorn sheep
gazing down at the about-to-be-nipped
grass.
I was crowned beauty queen in anticipation
of my father's clean decapitation,

pushed my baby sister's head under her
Saturday night bath, and hung my
heroin-addicted neck with a lamp cord.
I drove one lane, black ice roads waiting for
that logging truck with my name on it
to come round the mountain when she
comes.
And I sit benevolently, eyes wide open.

V

I am growing old with a cup of joe.
I am looking through the plate glass
    window of the *Hoi Chin-Koiti-O Snklip*
    Mission where they serve blue plate
    fry bread and smoked salmon.
I am on the Good Ship Lollipop, in Pig
    Hollow, and on Rock Candy
    Mountain.
I am a barrel rolling raven.
I am a fey-lost *thevsh*i.
I am a desolation angel.
And I am a Vitality of the Unborn.

I ran as a child down the aisles of America's
    churches screaming, "It's all a lie!"
I chanted *"hare krsna"* on Craig and Pearl
    Streets, washed in the White River and
    Porter Creek, incanted "give us our
    daily bread" on West Young and Fifth
    Avenues, and said goodbye on East
    Wellesley and Florence Lane.
I replied, "I am," after someone said, "No
    one's a loser."
I felt lonely and got married, did the right
    thing and got married, and did the
    wrong thing and got married.
I drove countless times past the corner of
    the eleven Roman crucifixions,
    October 27, 2018.
I stood peering six feet down wanting to
    take the next step.
I bought brass finger cymbals in a hole-in-
    the-wall shop on Pittsburgh's Market
    Square, all the while being told most
    emphatically, if threateningly, the
    really childish uselessness, so

subversive, the what-are-you-trying-to-
prove? of it all, but me thinking, quite
frankly my dear, I really do give a
damn, all the while trusting in the
great big Rrromantic, Swedenborgian,
Blakean, Kerouacian, not drunk on
wine, at least not much, of it all, but
drunk on what America could be,
should be, must be, and not an
America all picked out and washed up
in some ditch alongside a factory
carcass, not a toxic, strontium-90
cancerous America, but an America
where free exchange is free and where
every tree frog and wood pee wee has
natural rights and where you and I
worship at the altar of Let It Become.
And I sit benevolently, eyes wide open.

The Belfast Bodhisattva

Hubcap Collection Plate

The panhandler extends
his collection plate,
a bounced-loose hubcap
from a '72 Ford Pinto,
and calls after a passing car,
"Grace ain't graceful, brother!"
He is the one
at the interchange
of Route 2 and Shady Slope.
He wears a T- shirt
with a cat costumed as Superman
and a baseball cap
with U.S.A. bedazzled in sequins.
His shorts are cut
from the American flag.

The Belfast Bodhisattva

after revisiting
Richard Brautigan's
"The Galilee Hitchhiker"

Belfast Patrick
drove
a Renault Dauphine,
cherry red,
with three-speed transmission,
right off
Five Mile Prairie.
The night before
he had a vision
of fins
inside fish eggs
reaching
out from their
mothers' wombs.
Stopping
at the edge of
the Little Spokane,
he threw in
a line.
Mister White,
a wise, old
mountain whitefish,
picked up
the other end.
"Long way
from Ireland?"
he said.
"Out of my mind
is farther,"
Patrick
offered up.
"Oh,

I don't know,"
Mister White mused,
"I got a
school here
who might smoke
that saint
in your
pocket."

The Government Forage Station

Patrick sat
with an old Spokane
in a derelict
window frame.
Once a government
forage station,
the skin had
fallen off
the carcass.
Only bleached ribs
remained.
Together, they nipped
on a brown bottle
of trade whiskey.
"I don't know
what to do ..."
Patrick said,
but the Spokane
interrupted him,
"I live in
a tepee.
My horses starve.
Kids throw
stones at me."
Then Patrick continued
"... or even
what to say."

Zenware

Patrick opened up
a hardware store
in Spokane, Washington
and put koans
on the shelves.
People would stop by
with plumbing problems
or with electrical problems,
what have you,
and say, "Hey,
you got any
H-10-8 bushings?
You know, half inch long
with an outside five thirty-
seconds diameter and a number
70 inside diameter.
One of those."
Patrick would send
the seeker
to aisle eight, "Dharma,"
to find

    THE WHEEL HAS
    100 SPOKES.
    THE CART HAS
    NO AXLE.

Stories began to circulate
about an unsavory incident
performed back in Patrick's
teens.

Ghost Piano

Patrick used to come
to our house and dance.
This was in 1980s Spokane,
back in the days
when I urban homesteaded
in front of the brick ruins
of a German noodle factory.
Edith Boehm would play
her ghost piano,
and Patrick would jig about
in the front parlor.
After I left this place,
the soot-brick house
was torn down along with
the Catholic church
across West Fifth Avenue.
The ruins became apartments
filled with nurses who worked
in the hospital to the left
and the one on the right.
Now Patrick comes during Lent
to the parking lot and dances.
Ash-marked nurses move to a tune
played on Edith's ghost piano.

Miles Stravinsky

for Beck

"Why don't
you come to bed
and drive
your nail
into this old cross,"
Sheelah said
showing off some leg
while Patrick wrote
cosmic letters
to the faithful.
Then he
flashed that angelic
smile
she knew so well,
lifted his crow quill,
and blew,
transfiguring the bedchamber
into the *The Rite of Spring*,
transfiguring the bedchamber
into *Kind of Blue*.

Social Media

Patrick logged
onto Facebook
and trolled a Fascist
and took a hit
on white widow.
The Fascist yelled,
   AMERICA!
   BEAT THE HELL
   OUT OF IT!
Then an advertisement
popped up
offering
a cosmic cruise
to an astral plane.
   SILENCE!
   FEEL
   THE SOUND!
Patrick decided to
take the cruise
but was stopped
at the border.
He was
tied
to a stake.
Charcoal briquettes were
piled
about his feet.
They were set
ablaze.

Facebook grave marker

really? it's just another loss
like all the others

Sermon of the Bin

Patrick came down
from Mount Saint Michael.
He walked west
over the 395 overpass,
past Rogers High School,
to the Grocery Mission.
He found
aisles spread out
before him and
shelves stocked
with salvaged cereal,
limited-life soda,
and misshapen fruit.
At the back
of the Mission,
he came upon
a bin of dented cans.
Right then and there
Patrick seized upon
a teachable moment
by saying:

Grace to the damaged;
yours is the underground economy.
Grace to the discontinued;
you will be displayed.
Grace to the bland;
you will be served.
Grace to you who seek
a sustainable market;
you will be exchanged.
Grace to the pure;
you will be the circle.
Grace to the nutritious;
you will be called
the children of the circle.

Grace to you who are
marked past-date;
yours is the underground economy.
Grace to you when people
poison you and
troll you and
send all sorts
of false memes
against you;
you will gain in value
because you're just like
the loss leaders of the past.

Radio Free Pentecost

"The stammering tongues
will learn to speak peace,"
Patrick said
and walked
into a butcher shop
on Smrti Street.
The butcher
had on display
a number of
analog-to-digital-conversion
tongues,
all cut
from sacred cows.
Patrick chose
a misshapen one.
He planned
to prepare it
for lunch,
his specialty,
a *shanti* sandwich
with pulse shaping
onions.

Graveyard

for Wilson

Patrick went
to a graveyard
posing
as a groundskeeper.
He liked the graveyard,
as it was
next to a river,
so he cut the lawn
with his Barlow knife,
ordered the fallen pine cones,
and turned on the sprinklers.
He then cast
the graveyard out
above the river.
A nice redband trout
rose,
leaped heavenward,
and took that
graveyard.
Splash!

My Son's Funeral

When I was old,
I buried my son
on a basalt cliff
above the Spokane River's
Bowl and Pitcher.
His mother and I
laid his body
in a barnwood casket,
the wood resurrected,
its materials taken
from a ghost farm.
His brother
started up the music.
It was rap and pop,
Charlie Puth
and Wiz Kalifa's
"See You Again,"
so American,
and in so being,
so appropriate.
>It's been a long day
>without you my friend,
>and I'll tell you about it
>when I see you again.
Looking about
I saw a yearling mule deer.
A breeze moved
among the tree tops.
A ponderosa pine cone
fell.
My son's just-freed soul
sat on the stone wall
of a mausoleum
just above his funeral.
Patrick joined him
for a smoke,

always Camels,
always filtered.

Spokane, Washington
July 2018

Your Life

on the anniversary
of Wilson's death

You are the needle
the breeze shook loose
from the jack pine
a second ago.
You fall
twirling
straight down
into the raspberries.
Sadness overwhelms me.
You lie at rest.

Coyot' skull blown off
like a trucker's cap. Patrick
dons it in the rain.

No Name Lake
Coronach

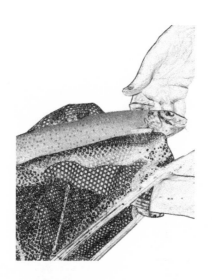

Epigraph

He is gone on the mountain,
  He is lost to the forest,
Like a summer-dried fountain,
  When our need was the sorest.

The hand of the reaper
  Takes the ears that are hoary,
But the voice of the weeper
  Wails manhood in glory.

Like the dew on the mountain,
  Like the foam on the river,
Like the bubble on the fountain
  Thou art gone, and forever!

Sir Walter Scott
"Canto Third, XVI"
The Lady of the Lake

1

Let's begin,
you and I,
father and son,
one living, one dead,
at the Forest Service sign,
the one posted
on the padlocked gate.

Recreation site closed
This site is closed for the FY 2018
recreation season

The following acts are strictly prohibited

- Entering or using this developed
recreation site or portion thereof
(36 CFR 261.58(b))

- Camping (36 CFR 261.58)e))

- Using a motorized vehicle
beyond the physical barrier
(36 CFR 261.54(a))

Blocked,
I back the tail-end
of our not-yet antique F-150
into the wood roses,
throw it into drive,
and spray dusty gravel
into the sticky currants.
"Fuck this," you say.
"Fuck the feds."

2

You came for cutthroat trout
on the lower jaw
two prominent, red slashes
> I came for a memory
> fly by
> at 270 miles per hour
> past my scribbles
that broad jump in the air
on the back and sides,
not red or gold,
but deep black spots
> that leaps out of time
> escape the square root
> of 2 X the gravity
> of your mass divided
> by your radius
into a cast-iron skillet
6, maybe, 22 inches
4 ounces, maybe, 6 pounds
> into a bone-lined well
> penetrate the silence
> of your absence
> in this shadow

3

Let's head on,
squarely resolute
and undeterred,
more than one way to snag a fish,
into the road's main channel.
You and I know a thing or two
about this patch of weald,
enough to head for
that shallow turnout,
this little eddy,
into which we slide,
that place
off the main road,
out of the deeper channel,
to find the second sign.

DAY USE ONLY
Area closed after sundown
and before sunrise
NO CAMPING OR FIRES
STRICTLY ENFORCED

"Fuck this," indeed,
and you and I
pull our door latches,
push and make
that can-opening sound,
and circle back,
you clockwise,
I counter.
We meet at the bed,
commence the unloading,
the disassembling and assembling,
using our present
roughly to prepare
for what comes next.

4

Not far below our feet,
below No Name Peak,
above the Lena Belle claim,
this place without society,
this place for lone wolves,
lies a 3,000 foot thickness
of dark-gray argillite.
This rock formed
during the Proterozic Eon,
metamorphosed
from aluminum and silica,
and calved from its supercontinent,
so called Laurentia
from so called Pannotia.

Back two billion years,
life was born
of aneorbic prokaryotes,
ancient microorganisms
with nucleus-free membranes,
some becoming
microscopic methanogens
producing far and wide
the world's first wee farts.

Along with these gassy little numbers
photosynthetic cynobacteria
began to kiss the earth
with oxygen,
    BMAA,
    alkaloids,
    cyclic peptides.
It's important to note
that some cheeks got pecked
with the kiss of death.

Then as if to prove
that size matters,
enter the eukaryotes,
those multicell behemoths,
our cousins removed
to the sempiternal power.

And it's one, two, three,
what are we living for?
Evolution seems so blind.
Next stop is humankind.

5

For you, tying on
has always been laborious.
You have no mind's eye
and rely on numbered steps
made of memorized words.
    Push through the eye
    of the rooster tail;
    reverse direction;
    loop around and under once,
    loop around and under twice,
    loop around and under thrice;
    reverse again to the first loop
    nearest the hook's eye;
    back through the loop;
    pull the ends tight.
    Set the hook keeper.
You gather up your gear:
    your polyester backpack,
    mesh-fabric trout net,
    3 tray tackle box,
    graphite composite rod,
    five bearing, cast aluminum reel.
Only then
you head off road.

6

Meriwether Lewis wrote in his journal
13 June 1805

the specks
      deep black
    instead of
          red or goald colour
    common to
          the U. States
long sharp teeth
      the pallet
          and tongue
a small dash
    red
      each side
    behind
      the front ventral fins

7

You descend

a rough, angled trail,
worn against the grain,
makes a precipitous drop

the black pine branches,
sharp and twisted,
cut the light into shafts

dumbly suspended dust,
a late summer winding sheet
creased by your descent

then, the encompassing circle,
No Name Lake,
erased by shadows

gear set down and line cast out
across the dead stillness,
and cast out and cast out.

8

What the cutthroat want:
    clear, cold water
    suitable substrate gravel
                less than 3.35 in
                in diameter
    water depth
                .5 to 11.8 in
    water velocity
                6.2 to 23.6 in/s

    submerged wood
    bolder cover
    cut bank
                mayfly pupae
                stonefly pupae
                caddis fly pupae

Line floats; bait dangles.
SLAM! so hard your soul breaks the
plane. I'm here. You're gone.

10

John Bourke, 1891, wrote in *On the Border*
    with Crook about General Crook,
    Commander of the Bighorn and
    Yellowstone Expedition

one hundred
                in one short afternoon

one hundred and forty-six
                another record
                      the 28th of June

over five hundred
                the total brought into camp
                      during the 28th

fifty-five
                the 29th of same month

trout
                men well fed

General George Armstrong Custer killed
    June 25 while Crook's command fished
    unaware on Little and Big Goose
    Creeks.

11

Let's end,
you and I,
father and son,
one living, one dead,
with your ascent
from the encompassing circle
along the rough, angled trail
through the black pine branches
and dumbly suspended dust.

Gravity pulls your gear.
A weight distends
your mesh-fabric trout net.

The last fish.

You do not smile.

Soon
you set down your gear
and part the netting.
Such a nice cutthroat:
fifteen inches or so,
the lean flesh toned
by survival,
the eye bright
with god-spark.

I smile.

Soon
I pull shut the door
and turn over the engine.
Such a nice cutthroat:
fifteen inches or so,
the lean fish fried

in butter,
the taste fresh
with god-spark.

Oh, my nice cutthroat,
too soon your soul will break the
plane. I'm here. You're gone.

Medicine Stick

General F.W. Benteen wrote in *Recreation*
  13 July 1895

I should mention that six troops
of the Seventh US Cavalry
of which I was then a captain
was in that section of country
to assist General Howard
in rounding up the Nez Perce.

Tired of my hexagonal bamboo rod,
my fly book being almost in tatters,
I had provided myself
with a long birch pole from the mountains,
a strong silk line without leader,
two large-sized Limerick hooks
baited with yellow and red winged
    grasshoppers.

Scene: Less than a week before the Battle of
    Canyon Creek where then Captain
    Benteen led the charge.
Later after the Battle of Bear's Paw, Chief
    Joseph asked to meet the buck-
    skinned, pipe-chewing officer who led
    his men into battle by waving his
    fishing pole.

I don't want to live.
Look, crimson ash berries on
a winter snowfall.

Epilogue

Táim sínte ar do thuama
agus gheobhair ann de shíor mé,
Dá mbeadh barra do dhá lámh agam,
ní scarfainn leat choíche,
A phlúirín is a aonsearc
is é am domsa luí leat,
Mar tá boladh fuar na cré uait,
dath na gréine is na gaoithe.

Anonymous
18th Century Irish keen

I am stretched on your grave
    And would lie there forever;
If your hands were in mine
    I'd be sure we'd not sever.
My apple tree, my brightness,
    Tis time we were together
For I smell of the earth
    And am stained by the weather.

trans. Frank O'Connor

BAD
TRANSLATIONS
OF MAX JACOB

What the Hell!

What the hell! The statues in the Capitol are under attack! The bronze Mother Joseph who extends her hands for cleansing pleads to me with her bronze eyes. You say I'm good with a hammer. If I put a nail through my sister's heels while putting up rafters, it was to grant her indulgence, and she looked forward to rapture through all her panic.

In the Spring Coulee

In the spring coulee, drought hasn't come and the gravedigger's shovel hasn't assaulted the earth. In the spring coulee from where the globemallows were exterminated, silent globemallows live in solitary.

In the spring coulee, the pools have lost their shade because the beavers have felled the water birch and cottonwoods.

In the spring coulee, there is a column that is stygian as stygian and behind the column is a bitterbrush that is in bloom, its petals of mustard and government cheese.

In the spring coulee from where the globemallows were exterminated, there are five leaping ń'týtiýáx, they are the five ń'týtiýáx of the šta?u?míx, and now the šta?u?míx comes without the ń'týtiýáx if at all and the ń'týtiýáx lie to get by.

ń'týtiýáx . . . Wenatchee-Columbian for
    salmon
šta?u?míx . . . Wenatchee-Columbian for
    rain

The Glitch Is on the Screen

for Beck

The glitch is on the screen; power failure. "Turn on the mantis-lens projector."

The boomeric cinéaste queues at the booth, only the smell of stale popcorn remains.

It glitches and the fantasiagraph runs for the viewers on the stream.

The avatar is eighteen years old. I sit down in the theater; others view the polarization of the mantis-waves.

"Finally, you've logged in!" the avatar voiced. "I suppose you'll chat during the fantasiagraph. Just click on the "view squad" button on the banner."

"Chat? Chat about what? emote my feelings?

Certainly not! Synthesize the flow of fantasy, the flow of the glitch, also the smell of those who queue with the boomeric cinéaste to build a brand of Reality.

I Saw

"I saw the best minds of my generation destroyed," said Allen Ginsberg. Why does it always seem to be the young ones who suffer? In the same opium den, they shoot up to open or close the doors of perception. You! who click along the dark web, let me read from The Book of the Dead. Hey, you, yes, you, the ones along Market Street, I recognize you! Ah, Caravaggio! And you, Basquiat. Look, over there, Thomas Chatterton with his pocketful of arsenic. Amy Winehouse lives a few doors down at 416, right next to my Chinese mailbox. Hébuterne and Modigliani tryst in the basement. And then there is you, young dumpster diver, who after the diabolical closing, plunges for the cole slaw and fried fish scraped from my well-appointed plate, you whom I don't know and are of no account, you for whom I counted 33 constellations along the city skyline; I dub you Mendieta.

He Didn't Know

He didn't know how to deal with the way she played with guns. When she pulled into the parking lot of the firing range, the pink camo-wearing freedom fighter, she pulled her assault rifle from its case, she knelt, sexted him, and then rattled off shots at the target. That Jesse Blue de Dorsoff was a cam girl, he thought that was hot, but that she had shredded the bullseye, well, that was quite another thing.

WHEN
HOOKER
BOOTS

First Thing in the Morning

"Meow."
I just wanted to say hi.
I have pancakes on the stove.
That's all I wanted to say.

Bone Sighs

To get to you
I had to wade
through a pool
of malt liquor cans,
spoiled condoms,
and bone sighs.

A plastic grocery bag
waved surrender
from a golden currant branch
like an "I Saw You" ad
in a free weekly.
    You weren't supposed
    to find me sleeping
    in this abandoned car
    in Peaceful Valley
    along the Spokane River.
    Thank you
    for helping me
    rub the blood
    from my knuckles.
Further on
a sign read

IF YOU
CAN READ
THIS
YOU'RE
IN RANGE

When Hooker Boots
Kick Raven
from Our Skies

I went out to a tavern
on Sprague and Napa,
down by a bend
in the Spokane River,
down by a bend
in Interstate 5.
The sun hung overhead.
You in hooker boots
stood at the curb, waiting.

The man behind the bar told me
his name was Nevermore.
After he poured me
a cheap, American draft,
I asked him,
"Do you like being a bartender
more than being a raven?"
"Truthfully," he answered,
"you guys give me more respect
than Poe ever did."

I knocked back the beer and
thought about Washington's Scablands,
the way its exposed basalt
had been powerfully transgressed
by ice age floodwaters.
And then I got restless.
I went back out to the street.
You were still there,
still standing at the curb,
still waiting, and
although I'm out of season,
when you wear those boots,
a load of your bird shot
always knocks me out of the sky.

for Patti Smith

Lacewing attracted
to u.v.a. light. Where am
I (you) in all this?

Facadomy

Let's fact check
to make sure it was you
at the Loco on Hangman Hill.
You were wearing this year's 504s
and a T-shirt with "Hostile Takeover"
emblazoned black on red.
Maybe you were waiting
for some banker,
or, at least, a guy on salary,
but I'm not sure,
because I'll bet
you really were looking
to flip some derelict property.
Hey, I'm open to gentrification.
Once under contract, you can
strip me down to the studs,
reroute my plumbing,
and re-plaster me
with hands of loving grace.
If you leave my brick facade,
it's a deal.
I've left the back door open.

The Divine Wind in the Cherry Blossoms

Tonight your fragrance
comes on the breeze.
You are my 桜,
and I am your 神風.
I settle into my Mitsubishi Mi-51.
I haven't the fuel to make it back.

$390,000 Evil Eye

after the sale of Shel
Silverstein's houseboat

Our bed is a dock,
and you, asleep, are
a houseboat moored
by the love ropes
we tied last night.
Your bathroom is sheathed
in reclaimed barnwood,
and you are plumbed
in scrap bronze
from a derelict,
1940s shipyard.
Your two storage areas are packed
to the low hanging rafters:
    palimpsest journals of Joyce Mansour,
    picture frames locking in sadness,
    and a necklace:
        cats-eye pendant,
        tarnished, on a woven copper chain,
        ragged-out.

I, too, am a houseboat,
but unlike you,
I have been cut adrift
by the city's property adjuster.
My hull floats offshore,
rent free,
among the other anchor outs.
Tonight my only hope
is this creaky rowboat.
The oars are instruments
I will use to work my way back:
    fountain pens of Andre Breton,
    oboe tunes infusing the new moon,

and dragonfly wings:
   pulse-blue veins,
   black on shame-weighted stigma,
   jitterbug.

Layla

for Jamie

A champagne raspberry
grows in my sun-bathed garden
like Layla's virgin heart.

If I don't eat
the golden-ripe raspberry,
Majnun surely will.

Haiku Instigatus

Wind. Clouds. A cat comes
into the room. Love follows.
A purr then a roar.

Meat. Burn. Hunger mounts
keenly poised to pounce. Thirst swells.
Then over the edge

Gracing the jet stream.
Oh! a ridge. Oh! Oh! a trough.
Subtropical waves.

Haiku Interruptus

The smooth stone cliffside.
The swift stream rushes below.
That one false step. Plunge.

Tight against the road.
The thrill of dangerous curves.
Snake in the road. Look out!

Please, just one more. All
good stuff congregates in threes.
But, alas ...

Second Thing in the Morning

Although
it's doubtful,
maybe, just
maybe,
it might be
possible,
if
the planets
align and
our moments
collide, for
just one more
pancake,
tiny, wild blueberries,
fresh-tapped maple syrup,
and a dollop of
double Jersey cream.

BLAKE'S
MEATLOAF

Imagine

I

"Imagine,"
Picasso said.

II

"Don't hang yourself,"
Picasso said
tying a brush
to the tail
of the barkeep's donkey.

III

"Opium has
such an intelligent smell,"
Picasso said
throwing a shovelful
on the painting hanging
from the ceiling.

IV

"Women are machines
for suffering," Picasso said
chopping their faces,
painting with bleach,
and sending the result
to an orphanage.

V

"It is a miracle
one does not dissolve
in the bath

like a lump of sugar,"
Picasso said
loading a blank
into the hand
of a toll officer.

VI

Picasso said,
"Steal."

Alana*

for Wilson after
Patti Smith

Every morn when I come alive,
see a bit of sun breaking through;
grab a ray, stick it with glue;
charge a battery against suicide.

Every morn when I am roused,
going t'pump that spark through your
        shroud;
I know that you're encased in mud;
pull the curtains, unleash the flood.

What I want, and I affirm,
is to light a fire to keep you warm.
I'll pluck down a shooting star;
make you a star on a marquee;
give you fifteen minutes of celebrity;
have you taste immortality,
tart, sharp pulse of blood,
then whisk you off to where it's sweet,
off into that Promised Land
where the lightning shatters through.

*child, a common transcription for
the Gaelic *leanbh*

Bullets Bottles Gravestones

on it
your name
lingering
somewhere
out there

Ghost Children

I have one.

The first conceived,
the first not born,
out of sight,
out of mind.
It is
a long way back
to the marriage bed,
to the hospital table,
the beginning desperate,
the end unspeakable.

And I have another.

The second conceived,
the second born,
too much with us,
poof in an instant.
Not long ago he
fished No Name Lake,
slumped in the final dark,
the living breathtaking,
the end unspeakable.

Yea, though I walk
through the Valley of Birth,
I will sing
a child's song.
This is the way
the word ends,
the word ends,
the word ends.
This is the way
the word ends,
not with a song,
but in silence.

Framing Medusa

It is 10:38 AM
in ironically red America.
My white, Fair Bianca roses
bloom like children's voices
to the left and
to the right.
With clippers in hand,
I deadhead the hips;
each litter-filled uterus
drops to the garden floor.
I wonder
about Georgia O'Keeffe's buds,
feminine,
timeless,
abstract beauty,
never a grub
never a planula,
never a tadpole
always a woman,
mother-tongue severed,
sometimes framed in gold,
too often framed in chain-link.

Blake's Meatloaf

I'm hungry, and
I've come
to the diner on Garland Street
for a plate of Blake's meatloaf.
I sit, and
the menu reads:
    Blake's heavenly meatloaf
    is lovingly sliced
    with hateful gravy and
    is hellishly accompanied
    with attractive potatoes
    in repulsive herb butter,
    good peas and
    evil carrots,
    reasonable pie
    with an energetic scoop
    of active ice cream,
    and a passive cup
    of Albion coffee.
The plate comes steaming
from the kitchen and
is set before me.
I cut.
I lift the piece
of Blake's meatloaf
to my mouth.
I chew,
I swallow, and
I think to myself,
"America's diners are built
from the stones of restaurant reviews
and its soup kitchens
from brimstone sermons."

I cut again, and
I lift another piece

of Blake's meatloaf
to my mouth.
The hellish gravy drips
on my hickory shirt.

Grief

Yellow tracks
of nicotine stain
run down
the bathroom walls.
Weed killer
and pesticides
grin empty-toothed
on the pantry shelves.
Standing for the bus
outside the grocery outlet,
an old lady waits,
her rheumy eyes
last night's downpour,
her shopping trolley
a corpse cat's yawn.

Deodorant Revolver

Your never-used
deodorant stick
is a revolver,
fully-loaded
with .38 special,
.58 grain,
XTP jacketed
hollow points.
It is
cocked and
sighted
on your
memory.
I run
a cold
shower.
I'm alone.

Chance Encounter

You were with your dog.
You told me
her origin story,
a rendezvous
between a dachshund
and a pit bull,
conjuring up images
of the Minotaur and the innocents
done in Krylon
like cave paintings
on some shooting gallery wall.

I was the one
next to you
with the Atticus letter bag
and iced whiskey,
I much older,
feeding off the youthful musicians,
the accidents in progress.
I told you, "No."

Soon
you will lie
on a surgical table,
a gunshot wound
to your testicles,
a fentanyl-filled balloon
falling from your ass.
Later,
stitched across the scrotum,
you will undergo a strip-search,
the prison guards
finding the balloon's twin.

And as for me,
I wish that

it were not so:
the algebra of need
not a Tiger tank,
a violent death spirit,
an ichneumon wasp;
the flowers of imagination
not a Bosch painting,
a silent obsidian muse,
a corpse plant.

In This Light

criminels et filles entretenues
circulent dans les souterrains
d'une grande ville,
à ouvrir les yeux
pour connaître notre héroïsme
    Charles Bauedelaire
    "De l'Héroïsme de
    la Vie Moderne"

Last night
walking through
manic bottle shards and
ragged songbird feathers,
you crossed the grocery lot
in felony flats.
You wore
a tie-dye-over-floral T
and combat shorts.
In mid-meth twitch
you shrieked,
"Release the hounds!"

Me? I'm no Baudelaire,
no extravagant green fairy
at *Brasserie des Martyrs*,
no fugitive dawamesk
at *Hôtel Pimodan*,
although standing
in the grocery lot's
frosty mercury-vapor light,
I thought you
a beautiful Magdalene
hideously hewn
from pentagonal basalt.

In this light

we, you and I, are bloodless.
Out of this light
we are ciphers
of silhouettes
who pass into box canyons
of serotonin badlands.
And I'd like to believe
that art can redeem us,
that one can redeem the other,
but as the sun comes up
tripping the photocell,
I fear what comes next:
a savage star,
our hothouse world,
an etiolated eternity.

We Used to Raise Hell Together

for Pablo Picasso
Angel de Soto
Fernande Olivier

Soon enough
the bill will come
descending from a moist cloud
and dangling on a delicate chain
woven from almonds,
the corpses of regretful cats,
and intimate memories.

for 2 sphinx moths	*10 sighs*
for scent of nicotiana	*30 sighs*
for 1 infant smile	*90 sighs*
Total	*130 sighs*